BECOMING
//
BLACK

FreeQuency

NEW ORLEANS 2015

Becoming Black
Copyright © Mwende 'FreeQuency' Katwiwa, 2015

Cover art by Sol Galeano (solgaleanoMgt@gmail.com)
Based on original design by Devin Reynolds

Layout by Geoff Munsterman
geoff.munsterman@gmail.com

second edition

*and this is for African immigrants who have considered assimilation
when your story is enuf*

❧

*it is a peculiar sensation this double-consciousness. this sense of always looking
at one's self through the eyes of others, of measuring one's soul by the tape of a
world that looks on in amused contempt and pity. one ever feels his two-ness—an
American, a Negro; two souls, two thoughts, two unreconciled strivings; two war-
ring ideals in one dark body whose dogged strength alone keeps it from being
torn asunder*

—W.E.B. DuBois

BECOMING BLACK

my father's lesson

Black father
tells daughter
that she is now
     Black

daughter is not convinced

she has grown up
in the same
brown skin
she sits in
as she listens
to Black father
tell her
of her newfound Blackness

but
Blackness

is something
her child mind
is not yet
able to understand

it jumps to
more familiar things
like
     cartoons

thinks to how the most evil of villains
are the ones
who dress in black
who shroud themselves
in the perceived terror
of its darkness

it jumps next to
     crayons

thinks to what it would mean
to start coloring
her family
with the same shade
once reserved
for the nighttime
and the monsters
that come out of it

daughter decides
she does not want
to become
        Black

she has yet to realize
that Black father
never gave her a choice

that Black father
was never given a choice

that he stumbled upon
this newfound Blackness
the hard way
how he heard it
in the hollow hallelujahs
that ricocheted
off the empty church pews
that were full
        until he sat down

it took just one year
in this country
for him to learn

that America shrouds
brown bodies
in the perceived terror
of their darkness
that it typecasts them
as the most evil of villains
scary

as both the night
and the monsters
that come out of it

he does not want his daughter
to learn of her own Blackness
in this way

so he tries to tell her of it

she is so young
he knows
she cannot possibly
understand what he means

and for now
he can't help but see
this unknowing

as a blessing

too black

white kids
in elementary school
always used to ask me
why I was so
          black

I didn't know

so
like children tend to do
when they are caught
in the snare
of not knowing

...I lied
I used to tell them

I drink so much chocolate milk
that it seeps through my skin
and stains it

or

once
I colored my whole body
with a black permanent marker
and now
I can't seem to get it off

or

once
when I was a baby
I was locked in a tanning booth
and this is how I came out
(never mind why I was in a tanning booth
as a baby)

or
sometimes

sometimes
on days
when I was didn't have the energy
to explain my existence

I would ask them
why they were so
        white

usually
they scoffed and said
that they
were just born that way

and I would
go quiet
and wonder
why I never gave
the same answer to them

and
whether
they would let it
be enough of an explanation
if I did

when the little white girl called me and Mo niggers

when the little white girl
called me and Mo
niggers

I didn't really know
what she meant

I had only known
nigger
as a dead word
buried deep
in the pages of history
decayed in the throats
of forefathers
that had been buried
with their language

her breath
blew the dust
from all the coffins
and unearthed
an entire history
reburied
into my body

when the little white girl
called me and Mo
niggers

Mo knew
exactly what she
meant

each syllable
tightened an
unseen noose
that had always
itched at
the back
of his neck

I watched as his
sixth grade smile
shattered
against the lunchroom table
her laugh   loud and
lined with hate shook
every last piece
onto the cafeteria floor
I don't think
I reminded him
to pick up the pieces
when it was all over

I was too busy
trying to figure out
how in one moment
I could know
so little about something
and in the next
know all about it

when the little white girl
called me and Mo
niggers

I felt her bark
grow teeth
and become
bite
a wound
that would go on
to infect
the rest of my life

me and Mo
were sent
to the principal's office
we hadn't actually
done anything
I had stayed seated
while Mo
yelled at her
from a distance

(there must have been
something passed down
Mo's bloodline
that made his bones
become boulders
and beg
him to remember
what happens
when Black boys
come too close
to white girls
with anything but
obedience on their tongues)

we sat
banished in that office
licking our wounds

and I
was left
feeling like
a soldier
in a war
I had just realized
I was fighting

not Black enough

to the Black kids
who made fun of me
for being
too black
and yet
never Black enough

the ones who
every morning
made sure
they reminded me
to brush my teeth
every night
(because how else
would people see me
when it was dark outside?)

the same ones who
never forgot
to remind me
before the day was done
that the only thing
whiter than the way I acted
was my teeth:

I give you my most
bitter and sincere
thanks

there were times I thought
I would never make it to see
the sun on the other side of
the tempest that was your torment

but in the end
you were the ones
who helped me fully
understand the lesson
my father's words
could never teach me

that Blackness
is less about
the becoming
and more about

the surviving

my mother's lesson

Black mother
tells
Black daughter

you must work
twice as hard as
everyone else
but only expect half
of what they get

Black daughter
listens

     but only

to half
of what
Black mother says

she learns
to work twice as hard
but forgets
to fraction
her expectations
each time she does the math
she realizes the equal sign
is a lie
and she has the audacity
to wonder why

they tell her
life is not fair

that it has nothing
to do with her
race or gender

that she should
lower her expectations

that success
is a slippery slope

and most people
who look like her
don't touch
the base of the mountain
so she should be
content with the view
from the cliff
she has climbed to

Black daughter refuses
keeps trying to climb higher
ignores the avalanche
of disbelief that threatens
to consume her

she is in the 4th grade
when she is first accused of
plagiarism
told that the words on the page
could not possibly be hers
could not possibly belong
to a little Black girl like her

hey little Black girl
who wrote this essay
on hate for you?
(if only they knew
how much
little Black girls
know of hatred
how they
learn to see
it in the mirror
instead of their
own reflections)

she is in the 10th grade
when *another* substitute
in an A.P. course
asks if she is in
the right classroom
the first time
she replied yes
through a tight lipped smile
the second time
she opens her mouth wide
and tells him
about himself

she is a sophomore in college
when a white boy
in the dining hall
asks her to serve him soup
because what else
would a Black girl like her
be doing on a college campus
except serving white boys like him

she is graduating college
with the highest honors
when she is told
she should not
celebrate herself

what do you have to
celebrate anyway
Black girl?
you only won those awards
because you are a
Black girl

Black daughter smiles
she can hear the dark humor
hiding in Black mother's lesson
finds it funny that
when she loses
it is never about
her race or gender
but when she wins
it can only be because of
her race and gender

Black daughter
celebrates herself anyway
she finally understands that
Black mother's lesson
is not one she will ever
truly be able to learn

but it is one
she will always have to live

embracing weakness

Claire Huxtable
is the only
positive image of a Black woman
I remember
from my childhood

the wife of a Black doctor
a mother to five children
and a law degree?
I mean
damn!!

this was superwoman
and I wanted
to be just like her

a few years later
I discovered comic books
predated
the Civil Rights era
I discovered no matter
how much I wanted it
that red 'S'
wasn't meant
for Black characters

then I discovered
the women that looked like me
were remnants of caricatures
Jezebels
        (who jumped from their towers
        and landed booty first
        in HipHop scenes)
Aunt Jemima Mammies
        (who took off their aprons
        and donned their crowns
         as Welfare Queens)

if only
we had a woman
to give to our daughters
as role models
we begged
and pleaded
lifted our faces
to the heavens
asking the gods
to send us the she
that we needed

when

LOOK UP IN THE SKY!
IT'S A BIRD!
IT'S A PLANE!
IT'S A STRONG BLACK WOMAN!

you know who I mean

a sista who achieves
by any means
but understands
the necessity of
putting her dreams
on hold
to uphold
the community

and this is the image we 'created'
to give our daughters
the strength
of superwomen

but it's tragic
when we pretend
to be the Picassos
of our painful past
because like scarlet "A's"
on women's bodies
to illustrate the romance
between sexism
and society
this symbol was
whipped
onto Black women's chests

until it bled
a red 'S'
on the wedding night
of racism
and sexual brutality

because like most stereotypes
the 'Strong Black Woman'
has her roots
in slavery's trees
just another character written into
the master's mythology
that went
a little something
like this

once upon a time
there were two women
both living in different hells
one was
the 'Strong Black Woman'
the other
the 'Southern Belle'

the 'Southern Belle'
was a white woman
oppressed
by Southern patriarchy

above all
valued for her chastity
she was bred to be a wife
but wasn't expected
to satisfy carnal needs   so
laying on her back
became another one
of the Black woman's duties

after all
she was strong enough
to take it

what strength
it must have taken
to work the fields
and the bedroom
unwillingly

what strength
it must have taken
to have children
knowing they were
Black oil
in the gears of slavery

what strength
it must have taken
to hide a breast
full of milk
from these same children
so the child of your rapist
could feed

to have survived
by becoming scapegoats
of American history
torn down in mind
and through the
exploitation of our strong
bodies

somebody tell me
how we managed
to adopt another one
of racism's
bastard children
held her high up to the light
but she was kryptonite
to our daughters survival
because
what the hell is the point
of teaching them to be superwomen

when they don't have
super powers?

Black women
have never been known
to stop bullets in our path
instead we're better known
for clutching our kin close
when we hear the guns blast

how can we
be deemed super
when we cannot even fly?
when we are history's
caged birds
who were never taught to sing
locked in cages
til we animorphed into
bird brained beings
chicken heads
'cluck clucking'
in video scenes
until flight became
a distant dream

what bitter irony
in comparing us
to a hero
with self-healing abilities
when in reality
Black women
are at the highest risk
of everything
from heart disease
to HIV

not to mention
the emotional pain
we shoulder
for our communities

and I don't know
the last time
I picked up a dictionary
but I do know this
quite well

there's either something wrong
with our definition of strength
or our definition
of self

the seven deadly American sins
a tribute to Trayvon Martin

of the
seven
deadly
American sins
being Black
has become
numbers
one through six

if this statement
strikes you as radical
you haven't been paying attention
I bet you were surprised
when the Martin verdict
came in and guilt
wasn't mentioned

and lets be clear

this was the Trayvon Martin case
George Zimmerman
was never on trial
he murdered a child
while we
were more concerned with
whether or not
a boy
had smoke in his lungs
than the fact that
he would never again
use them

I wonder
if his grave
bears his name
or if
it simply states:
this . could . have . been . you

I wonder
if they replaced
'rest in peace'

with

*'no justice
no peace'*

or if they knew
it wouldn't be true

when the verdict came in
people claimed
they couldn't stand it
but apparently
they couldn't stand
against it either
millions of 'Trayvon tweets'
and Facebook messages
calls for vigils
and moments of silence
but in the midst of it all
not a single riot

the N.A.A.C.P.
hailed this
as a sign of
'discipline'
I wager
it's a sign that
Americans weren't listening

all over the nation
people claimed
this wasn't an issue of race
that the outcome was

       "legally on-par"

accusing the
left-leaning
liberal
blackjack dealers
of once again
playing the race card

they asked

what would've happened
if Zimmerman were Black?
 would things have been
any different?

of course they'd be different
if Zimmerman were Black
this would have ended
with a prison sentence
you can ask Marissa Alexander
about any specifics
I'm missing
because she was sentenced
to more years in prison
than Trayvon Martin spent
on this planet

we live in a world
where a man can be
set free after admitting
to the slaying
of an unarmed teen

and CBS news
has the audacity
to run a piece headlined
by Zimmerman's brother
stating that
George would now
spend the rest of his life
looking over his shoulder
because

there are people
who would want to
take the law
into their own hands

it's funny
how some things are so
Black and white
while others
just taste like the rainbow

red
  like the blood that stained the sidewalk
  where he fell after being profiled
  for walking
  too slowly

yellow
  for the sun of Tracy and Sybrina
  that shone bright by day
  but by night had stopped glowing

green
  for the grass stains on pants
  that hung so low
  they heightened sensitivities
  without knowing

brown
  for the identity Zimmerman played up
  for the all white
  (*sorry – there was one Latina
  so that's what we now consider
  a diverse)
  jury

white
  for the privilege Zimmerman wore
  when he was out
  doing his neighborhood patrolling

and Black?
  Black is just another name
  for numbers
  one through six
  of America's
  seven deadly sins

the seventh was ever believing
we would find justice
in the hands of a system
that brought about

the oppression
of the Native Americans
the enslavement
of African people
carried out forced deportations
(even though we all know who's really illegal)
they gave summer camps to the Japanese—
who needs internships

when you have internment?
who needs lower unemployment
when we have prisons that turn profits?
we don't need to fear God
when we have capitalism to worship
and we certainly don't need
these assholes
always getting away
in our neighborhoods
so watch it

WATCH
IT

I was watching
a trial that was over
long before it could begin
so when the verdict finally came in
all I could hear
were the words
of the late Dr. King
calling for us
to not allow
the deafening noise
of injustice'
to drown out
the sounds
of freedom's ring

so in honor of his legacy
I ask you this one thing
to please join in this final call to

let freedom ring

let freedom ring
from the rushing rivers of melanin
that have overflown
into our streams of consciousness
to dilute the truth
so that people now claim
we live in a post racial society

let freedom ring

let freedom ring
from the meeting tables

of self appointed
gun totting
concrete cowboys
found in the ranks
of your neighborhood watch
or is it
your neighborhood NRA

let freedom ring

let freedom ring
from the graves of
Emmett Till
    Fred Hampton
        Sean Bell
           Amadou Diallo
      Oscar Grant
   Trayvon Martin
Jordan Russell Davis

and all the other brothas
whose names we will never know
because even in 2013
a Black man being killed
still
isn't enough
to make it onto the evening news

let freedom ring
let freedom ring

I said

LET FREEDOM RING

free at last
free at last

dear God Almighty

this is not the freedom
for which we've asked

the joys of motherhood

I've always wanted
to be a mother

growing up
I heard all about
'the joys of motherhood'
from the first day of school
to watching my kids graduate
I even looked forward
to the apprehension
of having them go on their first dates
I knew I was young
but I figured
it couldn't hurt to start planning
for something
so big
so early

but now
I'm 23 years old
and I don't know
if I have what it takes
to stomach motherhood
in this country

over the years
America has taught me
more about parenting
than any book on the subject

has taught me
how some women
give birth to babies
and others
to suspects

has taught me
that this body will birth kin
who are more likely to be held

in prison cells
than to hold
college degrees

there is something
about being Black in America
that has made motherhood seem

      complicated

seem like
I don't know what to do
to raise my kids right
and keep them alive

do I tell my son
not to steal
because it is wrong
or because
they will use it
to justify his death?

do I tell him
that even if he pays
for his skittles and iced tea
there will still be those
in the neighborhood
who will watch him
and see

criminal before child?
who will call the police
and not wait for them to come

      do I even want
      the police to come?

too many Sean Bells
go off in my head
when I consider calling 9-1-1
I will not take it for Oscar Granted
that they will not come
and kill my son

we may have gotten rid of the nooses
but I still consider it
lynching
when they murder Black boys
and leave their bodies
to rot
in the sun
as a historical reminder
that there is something
about being Black in America
that has made motherhood sound like

mourning

sound like
one morning
I could wake up
and see my son
as a repeat
of last week's story

sound like
I could wake up
and realize
the death of my daughter
wouldn't even be newsworthy

you can't tell me Renisha McBride
is the only
Black woman
whose violence
deserved more than our silence
what about our other
dark skinned daughters
in distress
whose deaths
we have yet to remember?
apparently
gender is not that great of a protector
if you come out of a body
that looks like this

there is something
about being Black in America
that has made motherhood sound like

      something I'm not sure I look forward to

I have written
too many poems about
dead
Black
children
to be naïve
about the fact
that there could one day
be a poem
written about my kids

but I do not want to be a mother
who gave birth
to poems

I do not want
a stanza
for a son
nor a line
for a little girl

I do not want children
who will live forever
in the pages of poetry
yet can't seem to
outlive

me

an open letter
to white feminists

dear white feminists

you keep asking

why can't we
bond over
womanhood?

but history has shown
this is not a bond
you consider
until convenient

you must think us
women
of short memories
and no inquiries
of our own

but did you really think
we would not question
your outstretched hands
when you made
our bent backs
bridges
to cross
to your
limited liberation?

that we would
forget
whose shoulders you stood on
to stand
eye to eye
with your oppressors?

who suffered
for your suffrage?

we
women of the margins
demand more than
an occasional invite
to a table that we built
and are still forced
to serve you at

you keep asking me
why we can't bond over womanhood
but you have yet
to answer my first question

Ain't I a woman?

when my white co-worker in college called me nigger part I

when my white co-worker
in college
called me
nigger

I did not
punch him
in the face

I did not even bother
to tell him of how
every bone in
both of my hands
begged to bruise
as they became
part of the breaking
of his porcelain body

I wanted to

        I wanted to
but then

I remembered
the confederate flag
that hung
above his bed
in his dorm room

in that moment
the unseen noose
that tightened
around my neck
choked my words
back down my throat
until they bounced back
into the muted mouths
of the bodies

a little white girl
once reburied in mine

when my white co-worker
in college called me nigger
part II

when my white co-worker
in college
called me
nigger

my white supervisor
asked me

did he say it
in a mean way?

I asked her
if it mattered

if his lack of anger
should have made me
hug him back
when he came
around the table
to say sorry
after he realized
he had crossed
a shaky bridge
he had already been
halfway across before

I wanted to tell her
that I had
sat up all night
wishing Mo was there
to help me lick my wounds

how maybe then
he might have reminded me
to pick up the smile
I left
shattered on the floor

and never went back for

when my white co-worker in college called me nigger part III

when my white co-worker
in college
called me
nigger

my Black supervisor
asked me

*did he say it
with an 'a' or an 'er'?*

I wanted to ask her
if it mattered

if changing the ending
of a word
could truly
rewrite the story
it had started to tell

instead
I laughed it off
and left her office

a few months later
she told me

that in the moment
before my laughter
she had looked in my eyes
and saw my face
become a stony facade
instead of eroding
beneath the
waves of tears
she saw crashing at the shores
of my eyelids

that when I got up to leave
she swore
she saw the bloated bodies inside of me
buoy me up from my chair and
f l o a t   m e   o u t   o f   h e r   o f f i c e

dear white people

*this poem is based on and takes lines from a Facebook post when
I asked Black people "if you could write a letter to white people…
what would it say?"*

dear white people
I don't even know
where to start

in between my busy schedule
comprised entirely
of surviving
white America
there is simply
no time
to write letters

besides
any letter I write
will most likely
bring tears to your eyes
and I
for one
have had my fill
of white tears

there are days I think
you are not worth my ink
that your whiteness
is draining me of too much energy
can't give you a taste of the tea
for fear
you'll colonize the whole kitchen

but today I am too angry to remain silent

dear white people
stop making everything
about you
and how
uncomfortable you are

I honestly
don't give a flying fuck
about your comfort level
you have made
my very existence an exercise
in discomfort

it is time for you
to make room at the table
better yet
go sit in the living room
I am not here
to coddle your feelings
not here
for your amusement

NO!
you cannot touch my hair
(this isn't a damn petting zoo)
and stop coming into
my office asking for the manager
as if
you aren't already looking at one

dear white people
stop telling me
about this 'color blind' society
you allegedly live in
telling me
you don't see race
is the racist drivel
I hope you choke on
telling me
you respect me
          and don't see my color
is like
telling me
you have to
pretend I'm not Black
in order to respect me

but let me assure you...

I
>   AM
>   BLACK

tho there are a plenty of things
I am not
like
>   your sassy Black friend

stop saying

*HHHEEEYYYYYYYY
GUUUURRRRLLLLLLLLL!*

when you see me

you are not that slick
I hear the way
you talk to Becky and Steve
everyday you sound like
vacation on Martha's Vineyard
where you spend summers
wading in the bitter blue
of the Atlantic
how I wish
my toes could touch the ocean
without stepping on the bones
of my ancestors

dear white teachers
why don't I know
who my ancestors are?

why is only one part of my history
important enough to teach?
for the love of God!
stop swiveling your heads
every time slavery is mentioned
NEWS FLASH!
I was not there

and just because
I am the only Black person
in this class
doesn't mean
you can ask me
to speak on behalf of my race
I'll believe you care about
the opinion of Black students
when you stop shutting down
classroom conversations on race
because I call a white student racist

dear white people
why do you hate being called racist
         more than you hate racism?
why do you listen to Tim Wise
         over actual Black people
         about the Black experience?

dear white people
stop using
'Black-on-Black' crime
as a reason
we shouldn't be outraged
by the murder
of Black people
by white cops

if a Black person
kills another
Black person
they will go to prison
and that is what we call
justice

if a white cop
kills a Black person
they will get paid leave
and that is what we call
justice

apparently
justice
is when
a Black body
dies

dear white people
every time I've written
'white people'
I've written it
in lowercase
because I am tired of you
capitalizing on our pain

we are angry
and raw
and tired
and angry
and raw
and tired
and angry
and raw
and tired
and tired
and tired

but we will not rest
because we know
the future belongs
to those who prepare for it

and you
have been getting us ready
for centuries

lessons on being an African immigrant in America

I
lose your accent
people will make fun
of the African girl
but nobody
            nobody fucks with the Black girls

        even when young
        they can be so

                angry

2
DON'T
stare
at
white
people

they are not animals
in the zoo

3
when they stare at you
like an animal in the zoo
do not be confused
do not bear teeth
when they reach out
to pet you
to touch your hair
without permission

you are   after all

so exotic
so foreign
so other

some will even call you
inhuman
they will call you
alien

they will ask you

who called your spaceship
to crash-land
your brain drain dreams
onto these Western shores?
these Western shores have
already landed ships
from your world
when we invaded it

but this is the 21st century
and we don't need chains
to make slaves
of people
anymore

4
with a name like
Mwende Kalondu Katwiwa
the jokes will come

do not envy
your brother
David
or blame
your mother
Lucy
the way their names roll smooth
off foreign tongues is proof
that colonization
and assimilation
go hand in hand

you
are your grandmother's legacy

5
when Black people tell you
...*you aren't really Black...*

remind them
how Amadou Diallo's
dead body
looked no different
than any other Black man's
in this gradual genocide
and I know
you may not call it that
in this country

but believe me
when I say
we know
what genocide looks like
we know
what it sounds like
it's white lies
telling families
they are enemies

we
are identical twins
separated at birth
now strangers
the hardest thing we will ever learn
is how to replant a family tree whose
fruits were exploited and
whose branches bore nooses

6
if people ask you if you're upset
because you're on your period
the week Al Shabaab
attacks a mall in your home country
do not marvel
at those who think
blood
only comes out of holes
the body has formed naturally

7
when nearly 300 of your
west coast kin
go missing
and Americans
claim them as

our girls

refrain from asking questions like

why did it take a month
and a hashtag for them
to claim family
when it was in the news?

or

why weren't the 60 schoolboys
attacked by Boko Haram
claimed as 'our boys' too?

instead
ask
that they do not
'Kony 2012'
these 234
to the backs
of their browsers

that they not be the kind of family
who only show up
to $12 weddings
and funerals

8
if you realize
you are powerless
to stop your metamorphosis
from the African girl
to the American girl
every time you break free
from Western cocoon
and fly back
to your roots

resist the urge to remain pupa
in the silk of stolen comforts
brace yourself
for the turbulence
that will shake your flight
with the truth

that you are no longer sure
which place is home
and which is more foreign
to you

my father's joke

one day
in what can only be described
as the sheer joy seen in a parent's face
when their children are old enough
to laugh at the pain
they have come to know
as simply
life

my father tells me

I have a joke I know you will like!

there is a Black person
and a white person
who are having a conversation

the white person notices something
on the Black person's shoulder
and reaches his hand out to him saying:

'there is something on your shoulder
here, let me get it for you'

the Black person
jumps back in alarm
and screams

'NO!

you white people are always trying
to take everything from us!!'

I burst into
a most dangerous
kind of laughter

the kind whose roar
I've learned to use
to drown out
the screams
of the bodies inside of me

not the bodies
who slip their stories
under my tongue
waiting for the retelling
with a patience
only accepting death
can teach

but the ones
who sometimes
with heavy steps
walk up my esophagus
slit my throat
and crawl out
to do the
telling themselves

acknowledgements

to my Mom: thank you for introduce poetry to me as something more than the writing of dead white men and depressed white women. thank you for all the quiet fight you have inside of you. you challenge me to be a better, more honest person and for that I will always be grateful

to my Dad: thank you for all of your support in everything that I do and who I have become in spite of what the becoming looked like. I am truly my father's daughter

to my brother Dave: I owe so much of my growth to you. I see that now. I don't know if you'll ever make it off the pedestal I put you on when I was 3

to my otha brotha Robby Jeune and especially my sister Kubby: thank you for being my biggest supporters, you have no idea how influential you have been in convincing me to following my passions

to my coach and next biggest supporter Akeem Martin: I know you have a bottomless arsenal of side eyes for me and all my crazy, but you still show up for me every .damn. time. I owe you so much

to my best friend and otha otha brotha A Scribe Called Quess?: you were the first one to truly listen to my stories and struggles with Blackness and living life in this body. without the hours you spent talking, listening and wondering what to do with the melting blob of feelings I became, I would not have been able to write this book

to Wildseeds: The New Orleans Octavia Butler Emergent Strategy Collective (especially Desiree and Soraya): you are helping me envision Blackness and myself into the future everyday. we are the universe's wildest dreams

and finally to Year of the Brown Girl (Alex Anita Anna Asia Ghiya Jordan Lauren Manali Sam F Samia Sherrill): you wonderful brown skinned women-goddess-warriors, you. thank you for holding me in a way I didn't know I needed to be held. thank you for helping me love myself in a way I never knew I could. thank you for being a forest with deep roots and MAD shade, I love you all so much